MW01130265

ALPINE ELEM. MEDIA CTR.
400 EAST 300 NORTH
ALPINE, UTAH 84004

DISCARD

EXPLORING COUNTRIES

Singapore

by Lisa Owings

BELLWETHER MEDIA · MINNEAPOLIS, MN

BLASTOFF!
5
READERS

Note to Librarians, Teachers, and Parents:

Blastoff! Readers are carefully developed by literacy experts and combine standards-based content with developmentally appropriate text.

Level 1 provides the most support through repetition of high-frequency words, light text, predictable sentence patterns, and strong visual support.

Level 2 offers early readers a bit more challenge through varied simple sentences, increased text load, and less repetition of high-frequency words.

Level 3 advances early-fluent readers toward fluency through increased text and concept load, less reliance on visuals, longer sentences, and more literary language.

Level 4 builds reading stamina by providing more text per page, increased use of punctuation, greater variation in sentence patterns, and increasingly challenging vocabulary.

Level 5 encourages children to move from "learning to read" to "reading to learn" by providing even more text, varied writing styles, and less familiar topics.

Whichever book is right for your reader, Blastoff! Readers are the perfect books to build confidence and encourage a love of reading that will last a lifetime!

This edition first published in 2015 by Bellwether Media, Inc.

No part of this publication may be reproduced in whole or in part without written permission of the publisher. For information regarding permission, write to Bellwether Media, Inc., Attention: Permissions Department, 5357 Penn Avenue South, Minneapolis, MN 55419.

Library of Congress Cataloging-in-Publication Data

Owings, Lisa, author.
  Singapore / by Lisa Owings.
      pages cm. – (Blastoff! Readers. Exploring Countries)
  Includes bibliographical references and index.
  Summary: "Developed by literacy experts for students in grades three through seven, this book introduces young readers to the geography and culture of Singapore"–Provided by publisher.
  ISBN 978-1-60014-986-3 (hardcover : alk. paper)
  1. Singapore–Juvenile literature. I. Title.
  DS609.O95 2014
  959.57–dc23
                                                                        2013050511

Text copyright © 2015 by Bellwether Media, Inc. BLASTOFF! READERS and associated logos are trademarks and/or registered trademarks of Bellwether Media, Inc. SCHOLASTIC, CHILDREN'S PRESS, and associated logos are trademarks and/or registered trademarks of Scholastic Inc.

Printed in the United States of America, North Mankato, MN.

Contents

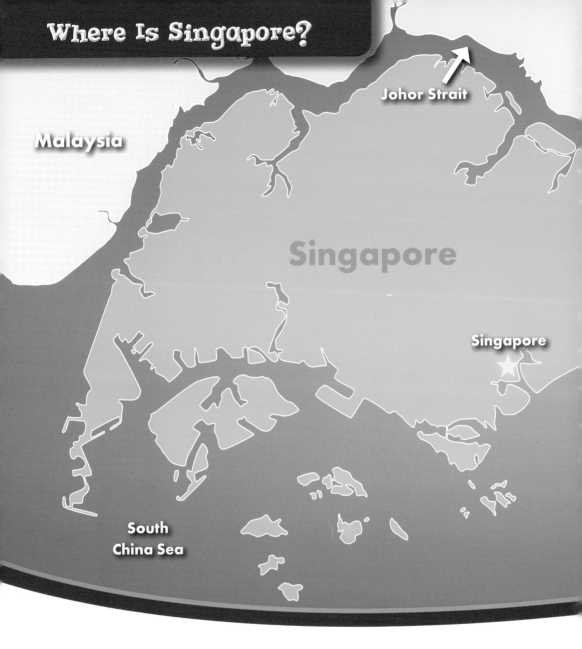

Johor Strait

Malaysia

Singapore

Singapore

South
China Sea

Singapore is a small island in Southeast Asia. It lies at
the tip of the Malay **Peninsula**, surrounded by some
60 **islets**. Singapore is a city-state. That means the
country contains only its capital city and the area
around it. The capital is also called Singapore.

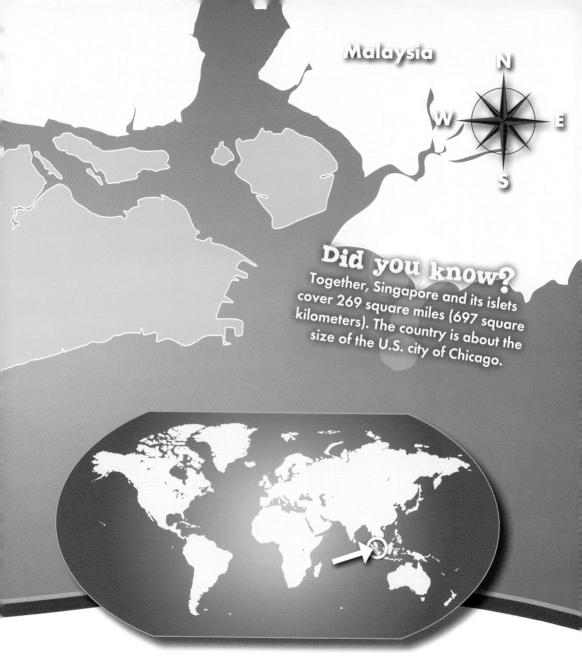

Malaysia

N
W   E
S

Did you know?
Together, Singapore and its islets cover 269 square miles (697 square kilometers). The country is about the size of the U.S. city of Chicago.

The country of Singapore is nestled between Malaysia and Indonesia. West Malaysia lies to the north across the narrow Johor **Strait**. Off Singapore's southern and western coasts are Indonesian islands. Parts of Malaysia and Indonesia also stretch east of Singapore across the South China Sea.

Rolling hills and **lowlands** make up Singapore's landscape. A cluster of low peaks crowns the center of the island. They include Bukit Timah, Singapore's highest point, which rises to just 538 feet (164 meters). Gentle hills and valleys dot southern and western Singapore. **Mangrove forests** fringe the northern coast and islets. To the east, the land flattens toward the sea.

Several short rivers flow toward the coasts. The Singapore River runs through the heart of the city before emptying into the ocean. Singapore lies very close to the **equator**. Because of this, the country has warm weather year-round. Rain falls most heavily from November to March. The dry season is from May to September.

Did you know?
Singapore has several human-made lakes. They hold large amounts of water for drinking and other uses.

MacRitchie Reservoir Park

The rounded peak of Bukit Timah swells above the rest of the island. Bare cliffs show where granite was once taken from its slopes. The old **quarry** is now a peaceful lake. On and around Bukit Timah stand the tall trees of Singapore's oldest forest. This **rain forest** is perhaps a million years old.

Trails winding through Bukit Timah Nature **Reserve** lead visitors under towering **canopies**. The paths are lined with ferns and thorny rattans. Birds and monkeys peer down from the trees, and butterflies brush past in search of flowers. Orchids, black lilies, and other blooms stand out against the greenery.

Asian
fairy bluebird

This crowded island still has room for a variety of
wildlife. Pockets of forest are home to long-tailed
macaques and the rare banded leaf monkey. Flying
lemurs soar from tree to tree, and bats take to the skies
at night. Pangolins in scaly **armor** search for insects.
In protected areas, tiny mousedeer scurry along the
forest floor.

clownfish

long-tailed macaque

monitor lizard

fun fact

Huge monitor lizards are at home both on land and in Singapore's waters. These lizards can grow up to 9 feet (3 meters) long!

The bright feathers of the Asian fairy bluebird and olive-backed sunbird stand out against the sky. Pythons and cobras slither across the ground. Off the island's coasts, **coral reefs** shelter colorful damselfish, wrasses, and angelfish. Clownfish hide inside sea anemones. **Corals** of all shapes and sizes dance in the waves.

Singapore is one of the most crowded countries in the world. Nearly 5.5 million people live on this small island. More than three out of every four Singaporeans are Chinese. They speak different **dialects**, and most practice Buddhism or Taoism. Malays make up the second largest group. Most speak Malay and follow Islam. The third major group is Indian. This group speaks Tamil and other Indian languages. Hinduism is a common religion among them.

Singapore takes pride in its **diversity**. The country has an official language for each major **ethnic** group. The languages are Mandarin, English, Malay, and Tamil. Singaporeans of different races and religions get along well. They all work together to help their country thrive.

Speak Malay!

English	Malay	How to say it
hello	apa khabar	AH-pah kah-BAHR
good-bye	selamat tinggal	seh-LAH-maht teen-GAHL
yes	ya	yah
no	tidak	tee-DAHK
please	sila	SEE-lah
thank you	terima kasih	teh-REE-mah KAH-see
friend	kawan	kah-WAHN

Did you know?
Singapore's government is known for making strict laws. However, most Singaporeans do not mind following them. They know these laws have helped make their country safe and successful.

Singapore is bustling and modern. It is full of tall skyscrapers and city lights. Nearly all Singaporeans live in high-rise apartments built by the government. Many people can walk to work or school. To travel farther, most Singaporeans hop on the country's high-speed railway. Others hail taxis. Wealthy Singaporeans drive cars through traffic-jammed streets.

Most children in Singapore do not have many siblings. Often both parents work, so grandparents or nannies care for the children during the day. Kids are encouraged to stay in school and get a job after graduating. Most live with their parents until they get married.

Where People Live in Singapore

cities
100%

fun fact

Buying a car in Singapore can be as costly as buying a house in other parts of the world. The government makes cars extremely expensive in order to lessen traffic.

Children in Singapore attend preschool for three or more years. Around age 7, they move on to six years of primary school. Classes are taught in English. Students also learn math, science, and another official language. During the last two years of primary school, children study for an exam that places them in secondary school. There are different secondary schools for different abilities and career paths.

Did you know?
Each Singaporean student is taught the official language closest to the one he or she first learned. Students are tested on this language at the end of primary school.

After four or five years of secondary school, students attend a school that prepares them for college or for finding a job. Most Singaporean students go to college, and many get advanced degrees. Some wealthy families send their children overseas to study.

Working

Where People Work in Singapore

manufacturing 19.6%

farming 0.1%

services 80.3%

Most people in Singapore have good jobs and make enough money to live well. About eight out of every ten Singaporeans have **service jobs**. Many work in banks and office buildings. Others work in hotels, restaurants, and shops to serve **tourists**. Factory workers make electronics, medicines, and other high-tech products. They also turn oil into fuel. The country's location on the water makes it easy to ship these goods to other countries.

Singapore has almost no farmland. However, a few people are able to grow beautiful orchids. Fishers catch some of the island's seafood. They also capture colorful reef fish. These fish end up in aquariums around the world.

Singapore offers sports, games, and activities for everyone. Nearly every Singaporean loves shopping at the city's malls and markets. While they are out, they dine at restaurants or open-air food courts called hawker centers. Singaporeans also enjoy going to concerts and movies. On weekends, families take trips to zoos, museums, or neighboring islands.

Singapore's sunny weather makes water sports especially appealing. People flock to beaches and waterparks for swimming and waterskiing. Soccer and **martial arts** are other popular sports. In *sepak takraw*, players hit a ball over a net using only their feet and legs. Indoors, people challenge one another to table tennis or *mahjong*.

fun fact

One waterpark in Singapore offers cable skiing. As many as eight water skiers or wakeboarders are pulled along by motorized cables instead of boats.

In Singapore, food is one of life's main pleasures. The diversity of cultures offers something tasty for everyone. Many Singaporeans start the day off with toast and coconut jelly. Rice and noodle dishes are popular for both lunch and dinner. Hainanese chicken rice is a national favorite. Seafood is common in many Singaporean dishes. Spicy chili crab is messy but delicious. Fish head curry is a spicy soup with a whole fish head in it.

Between meals, Singaporeans love to snack. Curry puffs are fried snacks filled with spiced chicken and potatoes. Another treat is *popiah*, or spring rolls filled with veggies. Dessert is often ice *kachang*. This is a mound of shaved ice drizzled in sweet syrup and other toppings.

fish head curry

teh tarik

fun fact

Singaporeans wash everything down with a frothy glass of *teh tarik*. Sellers mix tea and condensed milk by pouring them back and forth between two containers held far apart.

Did you know?

The Hungry Ghost Festival takes place in late summer, when Singaporeans believe spirits roam the land. People set out plates of food and put on theater performances to entertain the souls of the dead.

Chinese
New Year

In January and February, Singaporeans celebrate
Chinese New Year. They dress in new clothes,
clean their homes, and visit with friends and family.
Children receive red envelopes filled with money. The
streets fill with parades, dancers, and food stalls.

Singaporeans celebrate their independence from Malaysia
on August 9. Crowds dressed in red and white turn out for
stunning parades, performances, and fireworks. October
brings *Deepavali*, the Hindu Festival of Lights. Thousands
of lamps are lit across the island to celebrate the victory of
good over evil and light over darkness. Also in the fall,
Hari Raya Puasa ends the Muslim **fasting** month
of Ramadan. Muslims pray and feast with their families.

Did you know?
Each glass dome in the Gardens by the Bay is larger than a football field. One contains masses of flowers and trees. In the other, a mountain of ferns and orchids is misted by waterfalls.

Singaporeans have worked hard to balance their **urban** landscape with natural beauty. Between the city's streets and skyscrapers grow lush gardens. The Singapore Botanic Gardens offer acres of **tropical** plants and bright orchids. In the Gardens by the Bay, giant tree sculptures and glass domes tower over forests, flowers, and lakes.

Gardens by the Bay

The greenery that adorns roofs and balconies is both beautiful and practical. The plants offer shade from the sun. This way, less energy is needed to cool the buildings. Singapore's gardens also capture and recycle water that would otherwise be wasted. Singaporeans have a vision of being truly surrounded by nature. They want their city to become a City in a Garden.

Fast Facts About Singapore

Singapore's Flag

The top half of Singapore's flag is red for equality and brotherhood. The bottom half is white for virtue and purity. In the upper left corner is a crescent moon, which stands for a growing nation. The five stars are for Singapore's five values. They are democracy, peace, progress, justice, and equality.

Official Name: Republic of Singapore

Area: 269 square miles
                                      (697 square kilometers);
                                      Singapore is the 192nd
                                      largest country in the world.

Capital City:	Singapore
Population:	5,460,302 (July 2013)
Official Languages:	Mandarin, English, Malay, Tamil
National Holiday:	National Day (August 9)
Religions:	Buddhist (33.9%), Muslim (14.3%), Taoist (11.3%), Hindu (5.2%), Christian (18.1%), other (0.8%), none (16.4%)
Major Industries:	services, manufacturing
Natural Resources:	water, fish
Manufactured Products:	electronics, chemicals, fuel, rubber, food products
Farm Products:	orchids, fruits, vegetables, poultry, eggs, fish
Unit of Money:	Singapore dollar; the Singapore dollar is divided into 100 cents.

Glossary

armor—a hard covering that protects the body

canopies—thick coverings of leafy branches formed by the tops of trees

coral reefs—structures made of coral that usually grow in shallow seawater

corals—small ocean animals whose skeletons make up coral reefs

dialects—unique ways of speaking a language; dialects are often specific to certain regions of a country.

diversity—the state of being made up of people from many different backgrounds

equator—an imaginary line around the center of Earth; the equator divides the planet into a northern half and a southern half.

ethnic—belonging to a group of people with a specific cultural background

fasting—choosing not to eat

islets—small islands

lowlands—areas of land that are lower than their surroundings

mangrove forests—thick areas of trees and shrubs along a coastline

martial arts—styles and techniques of fighting and self-defense

peninsula—a section of land that extends out from a larger piece of land and is almost completely surrounded by water

quarry—a place where stone is dug from the earth

rain forest—a thick, green forest that receives a lot of rain

reserve—a protected area of land where animals and plants cannot be harmed

service jobs—jobs that perform tasks for people or businesses

strait—a narrow stretch of water that connects two larger bodies of water

tourists—people who travel to visit another place

tropical—part of the tropics; the tropics is a hot, rainy region near the equator.

urban—relating to cites and city life

To Learn More

AT THE LIBRARY

Bankston, John. *We Visit Singapore*. Hockessin, Del.: Mitchell Lane Publishers, 2013.

Layton, Lesley, Pang Guek Cheng, and Jo-Ann Spilling. *Singapore*. New York, N.Y.: Marshall Cavendish Benchmark, 2012.

Taylor, Di. *Singapore Children's Favourite Stories*. Singapore: Periplus, 2003.

ON THE WEB
Learning more about Singapore is as easy as 1, 2, 3.

1. Go to www.factsurfer.com.

2. Enter "Singapore" into the search box.

3. Click the "Surf" button and you will see a list of related web sites.

With factsurfer.com, finding more information is just a click away.

Index

The images in this book are reproduced through the courtesy of: TommL, front cover (top); Maisei Raman, front cover (bottom), p. 28; fotoVoyager, p. 6; spintheday/ Getty Images, p. 7; Klaus Vedfelt/ Getty Images, p. 8; Iwansntu, p. 9; mooinblack, pp. 10-11; Kletr, p. 11 (top); nvelichko, p. 11 (middle); artemisphoto, p. 11 (bottom); Then Chih Wey/ Photoshot, p. 12; catchlights_sg, p. 14; tonyoquias, p. 15; Ray Chua/ AP Images, pp. 16-17; joyt, p. 18; Schifres Lucas/ Abaca/ Newscom, p. 19 (left); Vincent St. Thomas, p. 19 (right); tristan tan, p. 20; Chen Ws, p. 21; Tibor Bognar/ Glow Images, p. 22; bonchan, p. 23 (left); Eldred Lim, p. 23 (right); Jonathan Drake/ AP Images, p. 24; toonman, p. 25; titlezpix, pp. 26-27; oilchai, p. 29.